IT'S TIME TO EAT POTATO SALAD

It's Time to Eat
POTATO SALAD

Walter the Educator

Silent King Books
A WhichHead Entertainment Imprint

Copyright © 2024 by Walter the Educator

All rights reserved. No part of this book may be reproduced in any manner whatsoever without written per- mission except in the case of brief quotations embodied in critical articles and reviews.

First Printing, 2024

Disclaimer

This book is a literary work; the story is not about specific persons, locations, situations, and/or circumstances unless mentioned in a historical context. Any resemblance to real persons, locations, situations, and/or circumstances is coincidental. This book is for entertainment and informational purposes only. The author and publisher offer this information without warranties expressed or implied. No matter the grounds, neither the author nor the publisher will be accountable for any losses, injuries, or other damages caused by the reader's use of this book. The use of this book acknowledges an understanding and acceptance of this disclaimer.

It's Time to Eat POTATO SALAD is a collectible early learning book by Walter the Educator suitable for all ages belonging to Walter the Educator's Time to Eat Book Series. Collect more books at WaltertheEducator.com

USE THE EXTRA SPACE TO TAKE NOTES AND DOCUMENT YOUR MEMORIES

POTATO SALAD

It's time to eat, let's gather 'round,

It's Time to Eat Potato Salad

A tasty dish is about to be found.

Potato salad, creamy and cool,

A picnic favorite, it's the golden rule!

The potatoes are soft, diced just right,

Cooked to perfection, fluffy and light.

Mixed with mayo, smooth and fine,

Each bite is like a taste of sunshine!

A sprinkle of salt, a dash of spice,

Some pepper, too, to make it nice.

Chopped-up eggs and celery crunch,

Potato salad's the perfect lunch!

Pickles add a tangy surprise,

They make us smile with wide-open eyes.

Mustard brings a yellow zing,

Oh, potato salad's the best thing!

It's Time to Eat
Potato Salad

Scoop it up with a fork or spoon,

A dish that's ready for morning or noon.

At picnics, parties, or at the park,

Potato salad is always the spark!

Sharing it with friends is the best,

This creamy dish beats all the rest.

One scoop, two scoops, maybe three,

Potato salad for you and me!

It's cool and smooth, a summer delight,

But it's just as tasty in the night.

Potato salad, so fun to eat,

A little savory, a little sweet.

Thank you, potatoes, for all you do,

You're a superfood through and through.

It's Time to Eat Potato Salad

With every bite, we cheer and sing,

Potato salad makes our hearts zing!

So grab your plate, let's have some more,

Potato salad's what we adore.

A dish so simple, yet so grand,

A perfect meal, just as planned!

When the bowl is empty, we'll all say,

"Potato salad made our day!"

It's time to eat, come take a seat,

It's Time to Eat Potato Salad

Potato salad is the treat to beat!

ABOUT THE CREATOR

Walter the Educator is one of the pseudonyms for Walter Anderson. Formally educated in Chemistry, Business, and Education, he is an educator, an author, a diverse entrepreneur, and he is the son of a disabled war veteran. "Walter the Educator" shares his time between educating and creating. He holds interests and owns several creative projects that entertain, enlighten, enhance, and educate, hoping to inspire and motivate you. Follow, find new works, and stay up to date with Walter the Educator™ at WaltertheEducator.com

www.ingramcontent.com/pod-product-compliance
Lightning Source LLC
La Vergne TN
LVHW052014060526
838201LV00059B/4026